CRYPTO CRIMES AND CAPERS

A THRILLING DIVE INTO THE DARK SIDE OF DIGITAL CURRENCIES

By

Michael McNaught

This book is an educational book for readers of all ages. Interested in learning about mischievous Cryptocurrency Escapades? Well, look no further. This is the book for you!

Copyright

Preface

Hi there! My name is Michael McNaught, a Scientist by profession, and an avid Blockchain and crypto enthusiast. I enjoy learning about cutting-edge technology and sharing my knowledge with others.

In "Crypto Crimes and Capers: A Thrilling Dive Into The Dark Side of Digital Currencies," we embark on a riveting journey into the underbelly of the cryptocurrency world. This book peels back the digital curtain, exposing a realm where innovation and criminal ingenuity collide.

As cryptocurrencies have revolutionized finance, they have also given rise to a new breed of crime. From notorious heists and Ponzi schemes to money laundering and illicit trade, this book explores the most infamous crypto-related crimes, offering a gripping narrative that intertwines technological genius with human greed and deception.

Each chapter is a blend of technological insight, criminal psychology, and real-world drama, aiming to educate and intrigue. This exploration is not just about understanding the crimes but also about learning from them. It's a cautionary tale that serves as a reminder of the need for ethical innovation and vigilant regulation in the digital age.

Table of Content

Introduction

Overview of Cryptocurrencies

Cryptocurrencies are a form of digital or virtual currency that use cryptography for security, making them difficult to counterfeit. The most defining feature of cryptocurrencies is their decentralized nature, typically using a technology called blockchain, a distributed ledger enforced by a disparate network of computers. This decentralization makes them theoretically immune to government control or manipulation.

The most well-known cryptocurrency is Bitcoin, created in 2009. Since then, numerous cryptocurrencies have been developed, including Ethereum, Ripple, Litecoin, and many others. These digital currencies operate on the principle of blockchain, where each transaction is recorded in a block and linked to both the previous and subsequent blocks. This creates a secure and unalterable chain of transactions, ensuring the integrity and transparency of the currency's entire transaction history.

Cryptocurrencies work through a process called mining, which involves using computer power to solve complex mathematical problems that validate and record transactions on the blockchain. As a reward for this work, miners receive cryptocurrency tokens, a process that simultaneously releases new currency into the system and incentivizes the network's security and maintenance.

For users, cryptocurrencies offer the potential for lower transaction fees than traditional online payment mechanisms and are operated by decentralized networks, not controlled by any central authority. This aspect appeals particularly to individuals who prefer transactions that might require some level of anonymity or security, beyond what is possible with conventional payment systems.

Despite their potential, cryptocurrencies also pose risks and challenges, such as their use for illegal activities, exchange rate volatility, and vulnerabilities of the infrastructure underlying them. As a result, they have become a subject of intense interest, debate, and regulation across the world.

The Appeal of Crypto: Benefits and Potential for Innovation

Cryptocurrencies have garnered immense popularity and interest for a variety of reasons, with their appeal lying in their innovative features and potential benefits over traditional forms of currency and financial transactions.

1. Decentralization: One of the primary attractions of cryptocurrencies is their decentralized nature. Unlike traditional currencies controlled by governments or central banks, cryptocurrencies operate on a decentralized network of computers using blockchain technology. This decentralization reduces the risk of censorship or interference from a central authority and can increase the resilience of the currency system.

2. Lower Transaction Costs: Cryptocurrencies can significantly reduce transaction costs, especially for international transfers. Traditional cross-border transactions often involve exchange rates and fees, while cryptocurrency transactions can bypass these costs, making them faster and cheaper.

3. Security and Privacy: The use of cryptography in cryptocurrencies ensures a high level of security. Transactions are secure, and many cryptocurrencies offer greater privacy compared to conventional financial transactions, appealing to users who prioritize anonymity.
4. Financial Inclusion: Cryptocurrencies have the potential to increase financial inclusion. They can be particularly advantageous for people in underbanked regions or countries with unstable currencies, as they provide access to a form of currency that can be more stable and accessible than their local currency.
5. Investment Opportunities: The rapid growth and volatility in the value of many cryptocurrencies have attracted investors looking for high returns. While this can be risky, it has contributed significantly to the popularity of cryptocurrencies as an asset class.
6. Innovation in Financial Services: Cryptocurrencies have spurred innovation in the financial sector, leading to the development of new financial products and services. These include decentralized finance (DeFi) platforms that offer financial services without the need for traditional financial intermediaries.
7. Smart Contracts: Technologies like Ethereum have introduced smart contracts, which are self-executing contracts with the terms of the agreement directly written into code. This innovation has potential applications across various sectors, from legal processes to supply chain management.
8. Empowering Creators and Users: Cryptocurrencies, particularly through blockchain technology, have enabled new ways for creators and users to monetize content and services, exemplified by

developments in areas like non-fungible tokens (NFTs).
9. Resistance to Inflation: Some view cryptocurrencies like Bitcoin as a hedge against inflation, particularly in countries where the local currency is unstable. Cryptocurrencies have a controlled supply, which can make them more resistant to hyperinflation.
10. Future Potential: The ongoing development and evolving nature of cryptocurrencies suggest a future filled with potential. Their capacity to integrate with new and emerging technologies, like the Internet of Things (IoT) and artificial intelligence (AI), hints at even broader applications and innovations.

The appeal of cryptocurrencies, therefore, lies not just in what they offer today but also in their potential to revolutionize various aspects of financial transactions and digital interactions in the future.

Setting the Stage: The Darker Aspects of Cryptocurrencies

While cryptocurrencies offer numerous benefits and have heralded a wave of technological and financial innovation, they also possess a darker side that cannot be overlooked. This shadowy realm is characterized by crime, deception, and a host of illicit activities, setting a complex and often troubling backdrop for our exploration.

1. Anonymity and Lack of Oversight: The very features that make cryptocurrencies appealing – decentralization and anonymity – also make them attractive for illicit activities. The difficulty in tracing transactions and the absence of a central

regulatory authority create an environment ripe for misuse.

2. Cybercrime and Hacking: The digital nature of cryptocurrencies makes them a prime target for cybercriminals. High-profile hacks of crypto exchanges and wallets have led to substantial losses of funds, eroding trust in the crypto ecosystem.

3. Ponzi Schemes and Scams: The world of cryptocurrencies has seen its fair share of Ponzi schemes and scams. The lure of quick returns on investments in a largely unregulated market has trapped many unsuspecting investors, leading to significant financial losses.

4. Money Laundering: Cryptocurrencies have been utilized for money laundering, allowing criminals to obscure the origins of illicit funds. The pseudo-anonymous nature of these transactions makes it challenging for authorities to track and apprehend the culprits.

5. Ransomware and Extortion: The rise of cryptocurrencies has been paralleled by an increase in ransomware attacks, where attackers demand payments in cryptocurrencies due to their untraceable nature. This has become a major concern for both individuals and organizations.

6. Darknet Marketplaces: Cryptocurrencies are the currency of choice on darknet marketplaces, where illegal goods and services, ranging from drugs to stolen data, are bought and sold. These marketplaces operate in the hidden corners of the internet, largely inaccessible to average users and law enforcement.

7. Regulatory Evasion: The lack of unified global regulation for cryptocurrencies allows for regulatory arbitrage and evasion, enabling activities

that might be illegal in certain jurisdictions to flourish in others.

8. Investment Volatility and Manipulation: The extreme volatility of cryptocurrencies has led to market manipulation tactics like pump-and-dump schemes, adversely affecting unsuspecting investors and damaging the market's integrity.

9. Terrorist Financing: There are growing concerns about cryptocurrencies being used to finance terrorist activities. The ability to send funds across borders quickly and anonymously makes crypto an attractive option for such illegal financing.

10. Legal and Ethical Gray Areas: The rapid evolution of cryptocurrencies has outpaced the development of corresponding legal frameworks, leading to numerous ethical and legal gray areas. This ambiguity can be exploited for criminal activities and poses significant challenges for law enforcement.

As we delve into "Crypto Crimes and Capers," we navigate this murky digital underworld, uncovering stories of ingenuity and deceit that shed light on the darker facets of the cryptocurrency revolution. This exploration is not just a tale of criminal exploits but also a critical examination of the vulnerabilities and risks inherent in this burgeoning digital landscape.

Chapter 1: The Birth of Bitcoin and the Shadow It Cast

History of Bitcoin: Origins and Initial Intentions

The story of Bitcoin, the first and most well-known cryptocurrency, begins with its mysterious creation and the revolutionary ideas it brought to the financial world.

1. The Genesis of Bitcoin: Bitcoin was created by an individual or group of individuals using the pseudonym Satoshi Nakamoto. The concept of Bitcoin was first introduced in a white paper titled "Bitcoin: A Peer-to-Peer Electronic Cash System," published in October 2008. This paper proposed a decentralized digital currency that could facilitate transactions without the need for a central authority.

2. Launch of Bitcoin Network: The Bitcoin network officially came into existence on January 3, 2009, with the mining of the genesis block (Block 0) by Satoshi Nakamoto. This block contained a message, a reference to a newspaper headline of that time, hinting at Bitcoin's intention to offer an alternative to the failing traditional banking systems: "The Times 03/Jan/2009 Chancellor on brink of second bailout for banks."

3. Decentralization and Trust: The key innovation of Bitcoin was its decentralized nature, achieved through blockchain technology. This digital ledger records all transactions across a network of computers, making it transparent and resistant to tampering. This system removed the need for a central authority, like a bank, to oversee

transactions, placing trust in a collective, verifiable process.

4. Mining and the Creation of New Bitcoins: Bitcoin introduced the concept of mining, where miners use computational power to solve complex mathematical problems and validate transactions. As a reward for their efforts, miners receive new bitcoins, introducing new currency into the system in a controlled, predictable manner.

5. Bitcoin's Libertarian Ideals: The creation of Bitcoin was influenced by libertarian ideals, particularly the desire for financial sovereignty and freedom from government control and inflation-prone fiat currencies. It was seen as a way to return power and privacy back to the individual.

6. The First Bitcoin Transactions: The first real-world transaction using Bitcoin took place in May 2010, when programmer Laszlo Hanyecz bought two pizzas for 10,000 bitcoins, a transaction that is now legendary in the crypto community for its staggering current value in retrospect.

7. Growth and Challenges: Bitcoin's journey has seen its share of challenges, including volatile price fluctuations, regulatory scrutiny, and debates within the Bitcoin community over technical aspects of the network. Despite these, it has grown in popularity and acceptance.

8. Influence on the Development of Other Cryptocurrencies: The creation of Bitcoin paved the way for the development of numerous other cryptocurrencies, each with its unique features and purposes, expanding the landscape of digital finance.

The history of Bitcoin is not just the story of a digital currency; it is a tale of a technological revolution that challenged traditional notions of currency and financial systems, introducing the world to the possibilities of blockchain technology and decentralized finance.

Early Missteps in Bitcoin's History: The Silk Road and Other Misuses

In the early years following its inception, Bitcoin, like many groundbreaking technologies, encountered its share of misuse and controversy. One of the most notable instances was its association with the Silk Road, an online black market platform.

1. The Silk Road: Launched in February 2011 by Ross Ulbricht, the Silk Road was a dark web marketplace that operated anonymously using the Tor network. It became infamous for selling illegal drugs, among other illicit goods and services. The use of Bitcoin as the primary currency on the Silk Road highlighted the cryptocurrency's ability to facilitate anonymous financial transactions, drawing significant attention to Bitcoin, albeit for controversial reasons.
2. Anonymity and Illicit Transactions: The anonymity afforded by Bitcoin was a double-edged sword. While it offered privacy and security to users, it also made Bitcoin the preferred currency for illegal online transactions. This included not only the Silk Road but other darknet marketplaces that followed.
3. Government Scrutiny and Legal Action: The association of Bitcoin with illicit activities like those on the Silk Road led to increased scrutiny from law enforcement and government agencies worldwide. This culminated in the FBI shutting down the Silk Road in October 2013 and the arrest

of Ross Ulbricht. The subsequent seizure and auction of the bitcoins associated with the Silk Road further brought Bitcoin into the public and regulatory spotlight.

4. Impact on Bitcoin's Reputation: The early use of Bitcoin for illegal transactions on platforms like the Silk Road tarnished its reputation, leading many to view the cryptocurrency primarily as a tool for criminal activity. This perception was a significant hurdle for the adoption of Bitcoin for legitimate purposes.

5. Regulatory Response: These incidents prompted a more vigorous debate among regulators and financial institutions about how to handle cryptocurrencies. It led to calls for stricter regulations to prevent the misuse of digital currencies while balancing the need for innovation and privacy.

6. Community Reaction: The Bitcoin community faced internal debates about the direction of the cryptocurrency. While some advocated for the absolute privacy and freedom Bitcoin offered, others sought to distance the currency from illegal activities and promote its legitimate uses.

7. Maturing of the Ecosystem: Over time, as the ecosystem around Bitcoin and other cryptocurrencies matured, measures to improve security and regulatory compliance were implemented. This included the introduction of Know Your Customer (KYC) and Anti-Money Laundering (AML) policies by cryptocurrency exchanges.

8. The early misuse of Bitcoin, epitomized by the Silk Road saga, played a crucial role in shaping the public and regulatory perception of cryptocurrencies. It served as a wake-up call to the

crypto community about the potential dangers and ethical considerations of this new technology, steering the evolution of the cryptocurrency towards more responsible and regulated use.

Chapter 2: Not Just Bitcoin - The Rise of Altcoins and Associated Risks

Introduction to Altcoins: The Emergence of Alternative Cryptocurrencies

As Bitcoin gained prominence and demonstrated the potential of blockchain technology, it paved the way for the emergence of alternative cryptocurrencies, known as altcoins. These altcoins were developed to improve upon or offer different features and use cases compared to Bitcoin.

1. Diversification and Evolution: The first altcoins started appearing around 2011, just a couple of years after Bitcoin's inception. These early altcoins, such as Litecoin and Namecoin, were often variations of Bitcoin, tweaking its original code to offer improvements in speed, efficiency, or to provide new functionalities.

2. Addressing Bitcoin's Limitations: Many altcoins were created to address perceived limitations in Bitcoin. For instance, Litecoin was designed to process transactions faster, and Ripple (XRP) was created to facilitate real-time, cross-border financial transactions for banks and financial institutions.

3. Expanding Use Cases: Altcoins have significantly expanded the use cases of cryptocurrencies. Ethereum, for example, introduced the concept of smart contracts, programmable contracts that execute automatically when certain conditions are met. This innovation opened up possibilities beyond mere financial transactions, including decentralized

applications (dApps) and decentralized finance (DeFi).

4. Innovation in Consensus Mechanisms: Altcoins also experimented with different consensus mechanisms beyond Bitcoin's Proof of Work (PoW). For example, Proof of Stake (PoS) was introduced as an energy-efficient alternative, where the chance of validating transactions and creating new blocks is determined by the number of coins held.

5. Increased Variety and Specialization: The altcoin market rapidly grew, leading to a diverse range of cryptocurrencies, each tailored for specific purposes. Some focused on enhanced privacy features, like Monero and Zcash, while others aimed at specific industries or applications, like VeChain for supply chain management.

6. The ICO Boom: The rise of Initial Coin Offerings (ICOs), especially around 2017, marked a significant milestone in the history of altcoins. Startups and projects used ICOs to raise capital by issuing their own tokens, leading to a surge in the creation and adoption of new altcoins.

7. Market Dynamics and Speculation: The proliferation of altcoins also introduced new dynamics into the crypto market, with increased speculation and investment opportunities. However, this also brought challenges, including market volatility and the emergence of fraudulent or low-quality projects.

8. Regulatory Attention and Challenges: The growing popularity of altcoins attracted regulatory attention. Governments and financial authorities began to scrutinize these new digital assets, grappling with how to regulate them without stifling innovation.

9. Mainstream and Niche Adoption: Some altcoins have achieved mainstream adoption in specific

sectors, while others remain niche, catering to specific communities or use cases.

The emergence of altcoins represents a significant expansion of the cryptocurrency landscape. It reflects the versatility and adaptability of blockchain technology, as well as the industry's continuous evolution in response to market demands, technological advancements, and regulatory frameworks.

Case Studies: Crimes Related to Altcoins

Altcoins, while innovative and diverse, have not been immune to criminal activities. Various schemes, particularly pump and dump manipulations, have been prevalent in the altcoin market. Below are specific case studies that highlight these issues.

1. Pump and Dump Schemes
   a. Example Case: 'Cryptocurrency XYZ' Pump and Dump Scheme: In this hypothetical case, 'Cryptocurrency XYZ', an altcoin with limited market cap and trading volume, became the target of a pump and dump scheme. A group of investors artificially inflated the coin's price through coordinated buying and spreading misleading positive news about the coin. Once the price peaked, these investors sold off their holdings, causing the price to plummet and leaving other investors with significant losses.
   b. Impact and Outcome: Such schemes cause market manipulation, leading to distrust among investors. Regulatory bodies often step in to investigate and take legal actions

against the perpetrators, but the
decentralized and sometimes anonymous
nature of cryptocurrencies can make this
challenging.

2. Initial Coin Offering (ICO) Frauds
    a. Example Case: The 'Promising ICO' Scam:
       A new altcoin, marketed as a revolutionary
       technology, launched an ICO to raise funds.
       The creators made false claims about
       partnerships and technological capabilities,
       collected millions of dollars, and then
       disappeared without delivering the product.
    b. Lessons and Consequences: This led to
       heightened regulatory scrutiny on ICOs,
       with authorities like the SEC in the United
       States issuing guidelines and warnings about
       ICO investments. It also prompted the
       crypto community to advocate for more
       transparency and due diligence in ICO
       projects.

3. Altcoin Exchange Hacks
    a. Example Case: 'AltExchange' Hack: An
       altcoin exchange, 'AltExchange', suffered a
       major security breach where hackers
       exploited vulnerabilities in the exchange's
       software, resulting in the theft of various
       altcoins worth millions of dollars.
    b. Response and Security Measures: This case
       study underlines the importance of robust
       security measures for crypto exchanges. It

led to a push for improved security protocols and the adoption of insurance policies to protect users' assets.

4. Decentralized Finance (DeFi) Scams
    a. Example Case: The DeFi Rug Pull: In this scenario, developers of a DeFi project based on an altcoin protocol created a seemingly legitimate platform offering high returns. After attracting substantial investments, they withdrew all the funds from the liquidity pool (a 'rug pull'), leaving investors with worthless tokens.
    b. Regulatory and Community Reaction: Such incidents have raised questions about the regulation of DeFi spaces and the need for more stringent vetting processes for DeFi projects.

5. Altcoin-Related Ransomware Demands
    a. Example Case: Ransomware Attack with Altcoin Demand: A company's systems were infected with ransomware, with the attackers demanding a ransom in a specific altcoin, chosen for its anonymity features. The company, faced with the loss of critical data, grappled with the ethical dilemma of paying the ransom, potentially fueling further criminal activities.

6. Broader Implications: This case highlighted the use of altcoins in cybercrimes due to their anonymity and ease of transfer. It sparked discussions on cybersecurity measures and the ethical considerations of meeting ransomware demands.

7. Privacy Coin Misuse
    a. Example Case: Use of Privacy Coins for Illicit Activities: Privacy-focused altcoins like Monero or Zcash, which offer enhanced anonymity, have been used for illicit transactions. An investigation uncovered a darknet marketplace where these coins were used for buying and selling illegal goods.
    b. Law Enforcement and Privacy Debate: This led to a complex debate between the need for privacy in financial transactions and the imperative for law enforcement to track illegal activities. It also prompted advancements in blockchain analysis techniques.

Each of these case studies sheds light on the different types of crimes associated with altcoins and their impact on investors, companies, and the broader cryptocurrency ecosystem. They also highlight the ongoing challenge of balancing the benefits of these digital assets with the need for effective regulation and security measures to protect against misuse.

Chapter 3: Hacking the Unhackable - Major Crypto Exchange Heists

Security Myths: Debunking the Myth of Unhackable Cryptocurrencies

One of the prevailing myths about cryptocurrencies is that they are completely unhackable due to their blockchain technology. However, while blockchain does offer enhanced security features, it is not impervious to all forms of cyber threats. Here, we debunk this myth by exploring various vulnerabilities and incidents in the crypto world.

1. Exchange Hacks: While the blockchain itself might be secure, cryptocurrency exchanges where people trade and store their digital assets are not immune to hacking. Numerous high-profile exchange hacks have resulted in the theft of millions of dollars in cryptocurrencies. Examples include the Mt. Gox hack in 2014 and the Coincheck hack in 2018.

2. Wallet Vulnerabilities: Individual wallets, both hardware and software, used to store cryptocurrencies can be vulnerable to hacking. Phishing attacks, poor user security practices, or software vulnerabilities can lead to unauthorized access and theft of funds.

3. 51% Attacks: This attack occurs when a single entity gains control of more than 50% of the network's mining power, allowing them to manipulate the blockchain. This can lead to double-spending, where the attacker spends the same digital currency twice. While difficult and expensive to execute, such attacks have occurred in smaller, less secure networks.

4. Smart Contract Flaws: For cryptocurrencies like Ethereum that use smart contracts, code vulnerabilities can be exploited. Inaccuracies in the contract's code can lead to unintended consequences, such as the DAO attack in 2016, where millions of dollars in Ether were siphoned off due to a smart contract loophole.

5. Sybil Attacks: In a Sybil attack, a network is overtaken by creating a large number of pseudonymous identities, allowing attackers to gain a disproportionately large influence. While blockchain networks have measures to prevent such attacks, they are not entirely foolproof.

6. Man-in-the-Middle (MitM) Attacks: These attacks occur when a hacker intercepts communication between two parties (like a user and a crypto service) and can lead to the redirection of cryptocurrency transactions to the attacker's address.

7. Phishing and Social Engineering Attacks: Cybercriminals often use phishing and other social engineering tactics to trick users into revealing their private keys or sending funds to fraudulent addresses. These attacks exploit human error rather than technological weaknesses in the blockchain.

8. Quantum Computing Threats: Although still in its infancy, quantum computing presents a potential future risk to blockchain technology. Quantum computers could theoretically break the cryptographic algorithms that secure blockchains, making them vulnerable to hacking.

9. API Exploits: Many cryptocurrency services use APIs for various functions. If these APIs are not securely designed, they can become a vulnerability, allowing hackers to access sensitive information or manipulate services.

10. Timejacking Attacks: In a timejacking attack, a malicious node manipulates the timestamp of a network's nodes, potentially disrupting the blockchain's operation and consensus mechanism.

While blockchain technology offers robust security features, the ecosystem surrounding cryptocurrencies - including exchanges, wallets, and smart contracts - has vulnerabilities that can be exploited. Therefore, it's essential to recognize that no system is entirely unhackable and to exercise caution and best security practices when dealing with digital assets.

High-Profile Heists: Major Exchange Hacks and Their Impacts

The cryptocurrency world has seen several high-profile exchange hacks, each leaving a significant impact on the industry. These incidents not only resulted in substantial financial losses but also shaped the regulatory and security landscape of cryptocurrencies.

1. Mt. Gox Hack (2014): Perhaps the most infamous crypto heist, Japan-based Mt. Gox, once the world's largest Bitcoin exchange, declared bankruptcy after admitting to losing around 850,000 Bitcoins (valued at approximately $450 million at that time). The hack exposed severe security flaws and mismanagement within the exchange and led to a prolonged legal battle for compensation, severely shaking the public's trust in cryptocurrencies.
2. Bitfinex Hack (2016): The Hong Kong-based exchange Bitfinex suffered a major hack resulting in the theft of 120,000 Bitcoins (worth about $72

million then). This hack led to significant changes in the platform's security measures and policies. Bitfinex issued BFX tokens to affected users, representing their losses, and later redeemed them, setting a precedent for handling such crises.

3. Coincheck Hack (2018): In a massive security breach, Japanese exchange Coincheck had $534 million worth of NEM tokens stolen. This incident led to heightened scrutiny from Japanese regulators, who enforced stricter industry standards and mandatory audits for crypto exchanges.

4. Binance Hack (2019): One of the world's largest cryptocurrency exchanges, Binance, lost over 7,000 Bitcoins (worth about $40 million at the time) to hackers. This breach didn't significantly impact Binance's operations due to their secure asset fund for users (SAFU), but it did lead to increased security measures and user awareness about safeguarding their digital assets.

5. KuCoin Hack (2020): Singapore-based exchange KuCoin was hacked for approximately $281 million in various cryptocurrencies. However, due to quick response and collaboration with other exchanges and blockchain projects, they managed to recover most of the stolen funds and enhanced their security measures post-incident.

6. Poly Network Hack (2021): In a different type of heist, the decentralized finance platform Poly Network was exploited for over $600 million in various cryptocurrencies, marking one of the largest thefts in DeFi history. Remarkably, the hacker gradually returned almost all the funds, citing the heist as a "security test".

Impacts and Lessons Learned:

1. Security Enhancements: Each hack led to a re-evaluation and strengthening of security protocols not just for the affected exchanges, but industry-wide. This includes improved wallet security, multi-factor authentication, and cold storage practices.
2. Regulatory Responses: High-profile hacks have often led to increased regulatory scrutiny and the development of stricter regulations and standards for crypto exchanges and wallets.
3. Insurance Funds: Some exchanges, like Binance with its SAFU fund, have set up insurance policies to cover potential losses from hacks, providing an additional layer of protection for users.
4. Industry Collaboration: Post-hack scenarios often saw increased collaboration within the crypto industry, with exchanges working together to track stolen funds and prevent their liquidation.
5. Community Trust: Each hack tests the trust of the cryptocurrency community. Exchanges that transparently handled the aftermath, compensating users and improving security, managed to maintain or regain user trust.

These high-profile heists highlight the ongoing challenges faced by cryptocurrency exchanges in ensuring the security of digital assets. They emphasize the need for robust security measures, continual vigilance, and proactive collaboration within the industry to safeguard against such threats. Additionally, these incidents have played a critical role in shaping user behavior, with more emphasis on personal security practices like using hardware wallets and being cautious of phishing attempts. The hacks also underscore the importance of regulatory frameworks that can provide oversight while fostering innovation in the rapidly evolving cryptocurrency landscape.

Chapter 4: ICO Scams - Dreams Turned Nightmares

Initial Coin Offerings (ICOs) are a fundraising mechanism used primarily by startups, particularly in the blockchain and cryptocurrency space. Let's break down what ICOs are and their initial promise:

1. Definition: An ICO is an event in which a new cryptocurrency project sells part of its cryptocurrency tokens to early adopters and enthusiasts in exchange for money today. These tokens may have utility within the project's ecosystem or represent a stake in the project.
2. Fundraising Tool: ICOs are a means of raising capital for startups. Instead of traditional methods like venture capital investment or bank loans, ICOs provide a way for these companies to raise large amounts of money quickly.
3. Token Distribution: In an ICO, tokens are sold to the public, often in exchange for other established cryptocurrencies like Bitcoin or Ethereum. These tokens might offer the holder various rights: equity, dividends, or, more commonly, access to a particular application or platform.
4. Market Access and Liquidity: ICOs can provide immediate liquidity for the tokens, which can be traded on various cryptocurrency exchanges. This aspect is attractive to investors as it allows for potentially high returns on their investments.
5. Decentralization and Democratization: One of the initial promises of ICOs was to democratize and decentralize funding. Traditional venture funding is

often limited to particular geographical regions and to investors who can afford large investments. ICOs opened the possibility for anyone, anywhere, to invest in an idea they believed in.
6. Regulatory Environment: Initially, ICOs were largely unregulated. This lack of regulation was both a blessing and a curse: it allowed for rapid innovation and fundraising but also made the space ripe for scams and fraud.
7. High Risk, High Reward: The early days of ICOs were marked by incredible success stories, with some tokens yielding astronomical returns. However, they also bore significant risks, as many projects failed to deliver on their promises, and the market experienced high volatility.
8. Evolution into STOs and IEOs: As regulatory bodies started scrutinizing ICOs, the landscape evolved. Security Token Offerings (STOs) and Initial Exchange Offerings (IEOs) emerged, offering more regulated and ostensibly safer alternatives to traditional ICOs.

In summary, ICOs emerged as a revolutionary way for startups to raise funds, offering high rewards but also accompanying high risks. They democratized investment in new technologies, though the lack of regulation initially posed significant challenges to both investors and authorities.

Notorious ICO (Initial Coin Offering) frauds have grabbed headlines over the past several years, underlining the risks associated with this form of fundraising is paramount. These scams not only resulted in significant financial losses for investors but also contributed to regulatory changes and skepticism towards ICOs.

Famous ICO Scams:

Here's an analysis of some famous ICO scams, how they occurred, and their consequences:

1. Pincoin and iFan

- How it Occurred: Pincoin and iFan, run by the same Vietnam-based company, promised high returns to investors. iFan was pitched as a social media platform for celebrities, and Pincoin claimed to offer an online investment platform. Investors were paid initial returns, resembling a Ponzi scheme, but eventually, these payments were made in tokens, not cash.
- Consequences: An estimated $660 million was scammed from around 32,000 investors. This scam highlighted the risks in unregulated markets and led to increased calls for oversight.

2. OneCoin

- How it Occurred: OneCoin, marketed as a cryptocurrency, was actually a pyramid scheme without a genuine blockchain. Its creators falsely claimed large returns and widespread usage possibilities.
- Consequences: The scam collected about $4 billion from investors worldwide. The founder disappeared, and several leaders were arrested, raising awareness about the need for investor education and due diligiFanence in ICO investments.

3. Centra Tech

- How it Occurred: Centra Tech falsely claimed ties with Visa and Mastercard to create a debit card allowing users to spend cryptocurrencies. Celebrity endorsements from figures like Floyd Mayweather and DJ Khaled brought visibility to the ICO.

- Consequences: The founders were arrested for fraud, having raised $25 million. This case brought attention to the misuse of celebrity endorsements in ICOs and led to legal actions against celebrities who promoted fraudulent schemes.

4. PlexCoin

- How it Occurred: PlexCoin promised an over 1,300% profit in less than a month, a clear red flag. It lacked transparency and operational details.
- Consequences: The U.S. Securities and Exchange Commission (SEC) intervened, halting the ICO. The founder was found guilty of fraud, and this case became one of the first instances where the SEC took significant enforcement action in the ICO space.

5. BitConnect

- How it Occurred: BitConnect promised extremely high and consistent returns through a supposed trading bot. It operated like a Ponzi scheme, paying old investors with new investors' funds.
- Consequences: When it collapsed, investors lost up to $1 billion. The BitConnect case is one of the most infamous crypto scams and significantly tarnished the public perception of ICOs and cryptocurrencies.

General Consequences and Trends

1. Regulatory Response: These scams have prompted regulators worldwide to scrutinize ICOs more closely. Bodies like the SEC in the USA started

classifying some tokens as securities, requiring compliance with securities laws.
2. Investor Caution: These high-profile scams have made investors more cautious. There's a greater demand for transparency and due diligence in crypto investments.
3. Market Impact: The exposure of these scams cooled the frenzy around ICOs, leading to a decline in their popularity and the emergence of more regulated alternatives like Security Token Offerings (STOs) and Initial Exchange Offerings (IEOs).

In conclusion, these notorious ICO frauds have had a lasting impact on the crypto industry, underscoring the importance of regulatory oversight, investor education, and the need for more stringent due diligence in the crypto investment space.

Chapter 5: Ponzi Schemes in Digital Clothing

Crypto Ponzi schemes operate using a framework similar to traditional Ponzi schemes, but with the added complexity and allure of cryptocurrency. Here's how they generally work:

1. Initial Setup and Attraction: The scheme starts with organizers creating a seemingly legitimate and often innovative cryptocurrency-related investment opportunity. This could be in the form of a new cryptocurrency, a trading platform, a mining operation, or any other crypto-related investment. The scheme promises high returns in a short period, which is the primary bait for potential investors.

2. Early Investors and High Returns: Initial investors are paid very high returns. These returns, however, are not generated through legitimate business activities or investment profits. Instead, they come from the capital contributed by newer investors. The high returns serve as proof of the scheme's success, encouraging the early investors to reinvest and attracting more new investors.

3. Dependence on New Investors: The scheme relies heavily on a constant influx of new investors to provide returns to the earlier ones. The organizers often encourage existing investors to recruit new participants, sometimes offering additional rewards for doing so, thereby creating a rapid growth cycle.

4. Lack of Transparency: There is often a significant lack of transparency about how returns are generated. Organizers may use complex jargon,

technical language, or vague explanations about blockchain technology and crypto markets to obscure the fact that returns are simply funded by new investments.

5. Sustainability Issue: As with all Ponzi schemes, the system is unsustainable. It collapses when the rate of new investment slows down and there is insufficient capital to pay returns to earlier investors. This can be triggered by market fluctuations, regulatory actions, or simply when potential investors become wary.

6. Anonymity and Cross-Border Nature: Crypto Ponzi schemes exploit the anonymity of digital currencies and the cross-border nature of transactions, making it harder for authorities to trace and recover funds. This anonymity also makes it difficult for victims to identify the fraudsters.

7. Exit Scam: Eventually, the organizers may execute an 'exit scam,' where they disappear with the investors' money, often blaming external factors like market conditions, regulatory actions, or hacking incidents.

8. Difficulty in Legal Recourse: Due to the decentralized and often transnational nature of cryptocurrency, legal recourse for victims can be challenging. Laws and regulations regarding cryptocurrencies can be unclear or vary significantly between jurisdictions.

9. The allure of high returns, combined with the innovative and technical nature of cryptocurrencies, can make crypto Ponzi schemes particularly appealing and dangerous to investors, especially those who are not well-versed in the underlying technology.

Crypto Ponzi Schemes:

There have been several notable Ponzi schemes in the crypto world, each illustrating the potential risks and complexities involved in cryptocurrency investments. Here are detailed accounts of a few significant cases:

1. BitConnect:
   - How it Operated: BitConnect was a high-yield cryptocurrency investment program, promising up to 40% total return per month. It involved a lending scheme where investors would use Bitcoin to buy BitConnect Coin (BCC) and then lend it back to the platform in return for interest payments.
   - Red Flags and Collapse: Critics noted the scheme's unrealistic returns and lack of transparency about how profits were generated. In early 2018, regulatory warnings and cease-and-desist orders from several U.S. states caused a panic, leading to a rapid decline in BCC's value. BitConnect shut down its lending and exchange platform, causing significant losses for investors.
   - Aftermath: The collapse of BitConnect led to legal actions against its promoters and a broader awareness of the risks of similar schemes in the crypto space.

2. OneCoin:
   - How it Operated: OneCoin was marketed as a new cryptocurrency with an educational

aspect. Investors were sold educational packages and received OneCoins in return. They were promised significant returns and incentives for recruiting new members.

- Red Flags and Exposure: There were early concerns about OneCoin's legitimacy, including the lack of a public blockchain and the emphasis on recruitment over actual utility. Investigations revealed that OneCoin functioned more as a pyramid scheme than a cryptocurrency.
- Aftermath: The scheme amassed billions before being exposed as fraudulent. Its founder, Ruja Ignatova, disappeared and is on the FBI's most-wanted list, while several other figures associated with OneCoin faced legal action.

3. PlusToken:
- How it Operated: PlusToken presented itself as a cryptocurrency wallet that would reward users with high returns for holding deposits in cryptocurrencies like Bitcoin and Ethereum.
- Modus Operandi and Downfall: It operated primarily in Asia and promised returns generated through exchange profits, mining, and referral benefits. However, these returns were paid from new investors' deposits. In 2019, several members of the team were arrested, and withdrawals from the platform were halted.
- Aftermath: The scheme was estimated to have amassed billions of dollars, with

significant impacts on the broader cryptocurrency market due to large-scale sell-offs of the fraudulently obtained assets.

4. MMM Global:
   - How it Operated: MMM Global, founded by Sergei Mavrodi, was a reboot of an earlier Ponzi scheme, MMM. It used cryptocurrencies as a method of payment and promised 100% returns per month.
   - Operation and Collapse: It relied heavily on a system of "Mavros" points and a global multi-level marketing network. The scheme gained a substantial following before it inevitably collapsed, as payouts exceeded the incoming funds.
   - Aftermath: The collapse led to significant financial losses for participants, particularly in developing countries where the scheme had gained a strong foothold.

These cases highlight the importance of due diligence and the risks of high-return investments in the largely unregulated world of cryptocurrencies. They also underscore the challenges regulators and law enforcement face in addressing fraud in the rapidly evolving crypto market.

Chapter 6: Ransomware - The Crypto Kidnapper

The rise of ransomware, a type of malicious software designed to block access to a computer system or data until a sum of money is paid, has been significantly fueled by the advent and proliferation of cryptocurrencies. Here's how cryptocurrencies have impacted the ransomware industry:

1. Anonymity and Untraceability: Cryptocurrencies, particularly those focusing on privacy like Monero and Zcash, offer a level of anonymity that is not typically available with traditional payment methods. This anonymity makes it difficult for law enforcement agencies to trace payments to the perpetrators of ransomware attacks. Even Bitcoin, which is less anonymous, still offers a degree of untraceability compared to conventional financial transactions.

2. Ease of Cross-Border Payments: Cryptocurrencies enable cross-border payments without the regulatory oversight and checks that exist in the traditional banking system. This feature allows ransomware attackers, who are often based in different countries from their victims, to demand and receive payments without the complications of international money transfers.

3. Decentralization: The decentralized nature of cryptocurrencies means that they are not controlled by any single authority, such as a central bank or government. This aspect makes it challenging for authorities to regulate or control these digital currencies, thereby providing a convenient financial tool for ransomware attackers.

4. Rapid Financial Transactions: Cryptocurrencies allow for quick and irreversible transactions. Once a ransom payment is made, it can be nearly impossible for victims to recover their funds, even if they don't get the decryption key promised by the attackers.

5. Microtransactions and Scalability: The ability to send small amounts of money across the globe at relatively low fees makes cryptocurrency ideal for small-scale ransom demands. This scalability has led to a proliferation of ransomware attacks, even targeting individual users and small businesses, not just large corporations or government entities.

6. Professionalization of Ransomware Services: The rise of cryptocurrencies has coincided with the professionalization of ransomware services. This includes Ransomware-as-a-Service (RaaS) platforms, where attackers lease ransomware tools and services in exchange for a share of the ransom, typically paid in cryptocurrency.

7. Increased Incidence and Sophistication: The convenience and effectiveness of using cryptocurrencies for ransom payments have led to an increase in both the incidence and sophistication of ransomware attacks. Attackers are continuously developing more advanced methods to evade detection and maximize profits.

8. Global Impact and Regulation Challenges: The global and digital nature of both cryptocurrencies and ransomware presents significant challenges for regulation and law enforcement. Jurisdictional boundaries and differing international laws regarding digital currencies complicate the efforts to combat ransomware.

In response to these challenges, governments and international organizations are increasingly focusing on regulating cryptocurrencies to combat illegal activities, including ransomware. This includes efforts to improve transaction traceability, enforce know-your-customer (KYC) regulations on crypto exchanges, and enhance international cooperation in cybercrime investigations. Despite these efforts, the inherently decentralized and global nature of cryptocurrencies continues to make them an attractive tool for ransomware attackers.

High-profile ransomware attacks:

Several high-profile ransomware attacks have occurred in recent years, highlighting the growing sophistication and impact of this type of cybercrime. Here are some notable incidents and their resolutions:

1. WannaCry Attack (2017):
   - Details: WannaCry was a global ransomware attack that affected over 200,000 computers across 150 countries. It exploited a vulnerability in Microsoft Windows and encrypted data, demanding ransom payments in Bitcoin.
   - Resolution: The spread of WannaCry was halted by the accidental discovery of a "kill switch" by a cybersecurity researcher. Microsoft also released emergency patches for outdated Windows systems. However, many systems remained vulnerable, and the total damage was estimated in the billions of dollars. The attackers were not definitively identified, though suspicions were directed towards North Korean hackers.

2. NotPetya Attack (2017):
   - Details: NotPetya initially targeted organizations in Ukraine but quickly spread worldwide. It masqueraded as ransomware but was more destructive, often leaving infected computers inoperable.
   - Resolution: The attack caused immense damage, particularly to multinational corporations. However, unlike typical ransomware, NotPetya did not provide a functional means for victims to pay the ransom, indicating its primary goal might have been disruption rather than financial gain. The U.S. and UK governments attributed the attack to the Russian military, but no direct resolution for affected victims was available.

3. Colonial Pipeline Attack (2021):
   - Details: This attack targeted the Colonial Pipeline, a major fuel pipeline in the United States. The DarkSide ransomware group encrypted data and demanded a ransom payment.
   - Resolution: Colonial Pipeline paid a ransom of approximately $4.4 million in Bitcoin to regain access to their systems. The U.S. FBI later recovered a significant portion of the ransom. This incident highlighted the vulnerability of critical infrastructure to ransomware attacks and prompted increased

government action and scrutiny regarding cybersecurity practices in essential services.

4. Kaseya VSA Ransomware Attack (2021):
   - Details: This attack targeted Kaseya VSA, a software used by IT management companies. The REvil ransomware group exploited vulnerabilities to deploy ransomware through Kaseya's network, affecting hundreds of businesses.
   - Resolution: Kaseya obtained a universal decryptor key, which helped affected businesses recover their data. The exact means of how Kaseya obtained this key were not fully disclosed. REvil demanded a $70 million ransom, but it was not publicly confirmed whether any payment was made. Later, REvil's online infrastructure mysteriously went offline, leading to speculation about government intervention.

5. Baltimore City Government Attack (2019):
   - Details: The city government of Baltimore, Maryland, was hit by a ransomware attack, which disrupted city services and operations for weeks.
   - Resolution: The city refused to pay the demanded ransom of about $76,000. Instead, it chose to restore systems from backups and rebuild its network, which cost millions of dollars. The attack led to significant improvements in the city's cyber defenses

and a broader awareness of the importance of cybersecurity in public sector organizations.

These incidents underscore the varied nature of ransomware attacks, from targeting private companies to public services, and the different approaches to resolution, ranging from paying ransoms to refusing and bearing the cost of recovery. They also highlight the ongoing challenges in preventing and responding to these sophisticated cyber threats.

Chapter 7: Money Laundering in a Digital Age

Cryptocurrencies have introduced new dynamics in the realm of money laundering due to their unique features. Here's how they are used in money laundering activities:

1. Anonymity and Pseudonymity: While not all cryptocurrencies offer complete anonymity, many provide a level of pseudonymity. Transactions can be conducted between digital wallets without revealing the true identity of the owners. Privacy-focused cryptocurrencies like Monero and Zcash take this a step further by obscuring transaction details, making them attractive for illicit activities.

2. Decentralization: Cryptocurrencies operate on decentralized networks. This lack of a central authority makes it challenging for regulators to monitor and control transactions. It also means that cross-border transfers can be made without the scrutiny typically applied to international banking transactions.

3. Use of Mixing Services: Mixing services, also known as tumblers, are used to obfuscate the source of funds. They mix potentially identifiable or 'tainted' cryptocurrency funds with others, making it difficult to trace the original source. While there are legitimate uses for privacy, mixers are often used to launder illicit funds.

4. Online Marketplaces and Unregulated Exchanges: Dark web marketplaces and unregulated crypto exchanges often transact in cryptocurrencies. These platforms can facilitate the exchange of illicit goods

and services, with cryptocurrencies being used as the medium of exchange. The lack of oversight and regulation in these spaces makes them conducive to money laundering.

5. Conversion to and from Fiat Currencies: Launderers may use cryptocurrencies as an intermediary step in the laundering process. Illicit fiat funds can be converted into cryptocurrencies, moved through various networks or services to obscure their origins, and then converted back into fiat, often in a different jurisdiction.

6. Initial Coin Offerings (ICOs) and Token Sales: ICOs and token sales have been used as a means to launder money. Criminals can inject illicit funds into these funding mechanisms, receiving seemingly legitimate assets in return, which can then be sold or traded in various markets.

7. Investment in Crypto Assets and Projects: Launderers might also use illicit funds to invest in various crypto assets and projects. The rapid appreciation in value of many crypto assets can serve as a lucrative way to increase the value of their funds while laundering them.

8. Peer-to-Peer (P2P) and Decentralized Finance (DeFi) Platforms: These platforms facilitate direct transactions between individuals without the need for a traditional financial intermediary. While they have legitimate uses, they can also be exploited for money laundering due to the reduced oversight.

Countermeasures and Challenges:

Governments and regulatory bodies are increasingly focusing on this issue, implementing regulations that require crypto exchanges and wallet providers to adhere to know-your-customer (KYC) and anti-money laundering (AML) guidelines.

However, the global and decentralized nature of cryptocurrencies poses significant challenges in enforcing these regulations. Coordination between international regulatory bodies is required for effective monitoring and control.

The evolving nature of blockchain technology and the emergence of new cryptocurrencies and decentralized finance platforms continue to present new challenges in the fight against money laundering.

While cryptocurrencies offer numerous benefits and innovations, their features also make them susceptible to exploitation for money laundering. Balancing the advantages of cryptocurrencies with effective regulatory measures to prevent their misuse remains an ongoing and complex challenge.

Tackling Crypto Related Money Laundering:

The global legal response to tackle issues related to cryptocurrencies, especially in the context of money laundering and other illicit activities, varies widely due to the decentralized, borderless nature of digital currencies. However, there has been a concerted effort in many jurisdictions to establish regulatory frameworks and guidelines. Here's an overview:

1. Implementation of Know-Your-Customer (KYC) and Anti-Money Laundering (AML) Laws:

- Many countries have extended existing AML and KYC regulations to include cryptocurrency exchanges and wallet providers. These laws require these entities to verify the identity of their customers, monitor transactions for suspicious activities, and report these to the relevant authorities.

2. Regulation of Cryptocurrency Exchanges:
   - Countries like the United States, Japan, and members of the European Union have regulations in place that require cryptocurrency exchanges to register with financial authorities. These exchanges must comply with financial services and AML regulations, including reporting large transactions and suspicious activities.

3. International Cooperation and Standards:
   - The Financial Action Task Force (FATF), an international body that sets standards for combating money laundering and terrorist financing, has issued guidelines for its member countries on regulating cryptocurrencies. This includes the "travel rule," which requires the sharing of information about the senders and receivers of cryptocurrency transactions.
   - The FATF guidelines have prompted many countries to revise their regulations to align with these standards.

4. Taxation and Reporting Requirements:
   - Tax authorities in various countries, like the IRS in the United States, have started treating cryptocurrencies as property for tax purposes, requiring citizens to report their cryptocurrency transactions and holdings, thereby reducing anonymity.

5. Banning or Restricting Cryptocurrencies:
   - Some countries, notably China and a few others, have taken a more stringent approach, banning or severely restricting the use of cryptocurrencies, particularly in relation to their use in transactions and trades. These bans often extend to mining activities as well.

6. Legal Frameworks for ICOs and Security Tokens:
   - Recognizing the growth of Initial Coin Offerings (ICOs) and security token offerings (STOs), several countries have either regulated or provided guidelines for these activities to protect investors and prevent illegal fund flows.

7. Decentralized Finance (DeFi) and New Challenges:

- As DeFi platforms gain popularity, they present new regulatory challenges due to their decentralized nature. Regulatory responses to DeFi are still evolving, with authorities examining how existing financial regulations can be applied to these platforms.

8. Ongoing Monitoring and Adaptation:
   - Given the rapid evolution of blockchain technology and the emergence of new forms of cryptocurrencies, regulatory bodies continue to monitor developments and adapt their legal frameworks accordingly.

Despite these efforts, the enforcement of these regulations remains challenging. The pseudonymous nature of many cryptocurrencies, the existence of privacy coins, and the decentralization of blockchain networks make it difficult to fully control and monitor all activities.

Moreover, the global nature of the cryptocurrency market means that regulatory arbitrage – where entities operate from jurisdictions with less stringent regulations – remains a concern. Global cooperation and harmonization of regulations are thus key aspects of effectively tackling the use of cryptocurrencies in money laundering and related illicit activities.

Chapter 8: Cryptocurrency and Terrorism Financing

Analyzing how terrorist groups might use cryptocurrencies involves understanding the attributes of these digital currencies and how they could be exploited for illicit purposes. Here are key points of consideration:

1. Anonymity and Privacy: Cryptocurrencies, especially privacy-focused ones like Monero or Zcash, can provide levels of anonymity that are appealing to terrorist groups. They can conduct transactions that are difficult to trace, providing a degree of privacy for funding sources and expenditures.

2. Global and Borderless Transactions: Cryptocurrencies operate on a global scale, independent of national banking systems. This allows terrorist groups to easily move funds across borders without dealing with traditional banking regulations or detection mechanisms that are in place for international money transfers.

3. Ease of Use and Accessibility: With the increasing availability of cryptocurrency technology, it's becoming easier for non-technical users to conduct transactions. Terrorist groups can capitalize on this ease of use to mobilize funds quickly and efficiently among a dispersed network.

4. Fundraising Through Crypto Donations: Terrorist organizations might use social media and other online platforms to solicit cryptocurrency donations from sympathizers worldwide, making it harder for authorities to track and intercept these funds.

5. Avoiding Sanctions and Financial Regulation: Cryptocurrencies can be used to circumvent economic sanctions and avoid the scrutiny that comes with using the conventional financial system. This could be particularly appealing for terrorist groups in sanctioned countries.

6. Use in Dark Web Marketplaces: The dark web offers various illegal services and goods, often transacted in cryptocurrencies. Terrorist groups could use these platforms for acquiring materials, false documents, or even recruiting members.

7. Laundering and Mixing Services: Cryptocurrency mixing services, which obscure the source of funds, can be used to launder money. Terrorist groups might use these services to clean their funds before using them for operational purposes.

8. Investment and Value Storage: Considering the volatility and potential for rapid value increase in cryptocurrencies, they could be used as a form of investment. Terrorist groups might hold cryptocurrencies as assets that can potentially appreciate in value.

9. Microtransactions and Crowdfunding: The ability to send small amounts of money internationally with relative ease could facilitate micro-financing of terrorist activities through a large number of small donations.

10. Potential for Creating Proprietary Cryptocurrencies: Though more complex, there's a possibility of terrorist groups creating their own cryptocurrencies to avoid any form of external monitoring altogether.

However, it's important to note that while cryptocurrencies offer certain advantages for illicit activities, they also have limitations. Most cryptocurrencies are not entirely anonymous; they operate on public blockchains where transactions are visible, which can be used by law enforcement to track and analyze patterns of illegal activity. Additionally, converting cryptocurrencies into fiat currency (regular money) often requires using exchanges that have Know Your Customer (KYC) and Anti-Money Laundering (AML) regulations in place.

Combating the Threat:

International efforts to combat the use of cryptocurrencies in terrorism financing are multifaceted, involving collaboration among governments, regulatory bodies, financial institutions, and international organizations. The primary focus of these efforts is to enhance regulatory frameworks, improve monitoring and reporting systems, and foster international cooperation. Key aspects of these efforts include:

1. Regulatory Frameworks and Compliance: Many countries are implementing regulatory frameworks to govern cryptocurrency transactions. This includes enforcing Know Your Customer (KYC) and Anti-Money Laundering (AML) regulations on cryptocurrency exchanges and wallet providers. Such measures aim to prevent anonymity in crypto transactions, making it harder for terrorist groups to use these platforms for financing.
2. Financial Action Task Force (FATF) Guidelines: The FATF, an intergovernmental organization, plays a pivotal role in setting global standards for combating money laundering and terrorist financing. It has issued specific guidelines for virtual assets and their service providers, urging

countries to enforce strict oversight over cryptocurrency transactions.

3. International Cooperation and Intelligence Sharing: Combating crypto-related terrorism financing requires robust international cooperation. This involves sharing intelligence and financial data among countries to track and disrupt the financial networks of terrorist organizations.

4. Monitoring and Analysis Tools: Governments and international agencies are increasingly using sophisticated tools to monitor and analyze cryptocurrency transactions. These tools help in identifying suspicious patterns and tracing the flow of funds related to terrorist activities.

5. Public-Private Partnerships: Collaborating with private sector entities, especially those in the cryptocurrency industry, is crucial. This partnership ensures that private firms comply with regulatory standards and contribute to detecting and reporting suspicious activities.

6. Capacity Building and Training: Developing the technical and legal capacity of law enforcement, financial regulators, and other relevant entities is key. This includes training in the latest technologies and methods used in tracking crypto transactions.

7. Updating Legal Frameworks: As the use of cryptocurrencies evolves, so too must the legal frameworks that govern them. This involves updating laws to cover various aspects of digital currencies and ensuring they are equipped to handle the unique challenges posed by these assets.

8. Awareness and Education Campaigns: Raising awareness among financial institutions, cryptocurrency users, and the general public about the risks of cryptocurrencies being used for terrorism financing is important. This includes

educating them on how to recognize and report suspicious activities.

9. Global Standards for Cross-Border Transactions: Establishing and enforcing global standards for cross-border crypto transactions can help in monitoring and controlling the flow of funds across nations, thereby preventing their misuse for terrorist activities.

10. Collaboration with Cryptocurrency Platforms: Engaging with cryptocurrency platforms to develop and implement features that can help in identifying and reporting suspicious activities. This includes the use of blockchain analytics and other technological solutions.

Overall, the international community recognizes the need for a coordinated, dynamic approach to address the challenges posed by the use of cryptocurrencies in terrorism financing. This requires ongoing adaptation and collaboration to stay ahead of the tactics used by terrorist groups.

Chapter 9: The Regulatory Battleground

Different countries have adopted varying approaches to regulating cryptocurrencies, reflecting their unique economic contexts, legal systems, and attitudes towards financial innovation and risk. Here's an overview of how some countries are handling cryptocurrency regulation:

1. United States: The U.S. does not have a unified regulatory framework for cryptocurrencies; instead, various federal and state agencies oversee different aspects. The Securities and Exchange Commission (SEC) treats certain cryptocurrencies as securities, while the Commodity Futures Trading Commission (CFTC) considers them commodities. The Internal Revenue Service (IRS) classifies them as property for tax purposes. Additionally, the Financial Crimes Enforcement Network (FinCEN) imposes anti-money laundering (AML) regulations on cryptocurrency exchanges.

2. European Union: The EU is working towards a harmonized regulatory approach with its proposed Markets in Crypto-Assets (MiCA) regulation, aiming to provide legal clarity and consumer protection while fostering innovation. MiCA focuses on stablecoins, asset-referenced tokens, and crypto-asset service providers, emphasizing transparency, authorization, and supervision.

3. China: China has taken a stringent approach towards cryptocurrencies. It has banned cryptocurrency exchanges and initial coin offerings (ICOs) within its borders. The People's Bank of China (PBoC) has been developing a digital yuan, a

state-backed digital currency, as part of its push to centralize digital asset control.

4. Japan: Japan is one of the more crypto-friendly countries, having recognized Bitcoin and other digital currencies as legal property under the Payment Services Act (PSA). The country has a registration process for cryptocurrency exchanges, enforcing strict standards for security and compliance with AML/CFT (Combating the Financing of Terrorism) regulations.

5. South Korea: South Korea has a dynamic cryptocurrency market, with the government implementing regulations to control crypto trading and reduce risks. These include AML policies, real-name account trading, and a ban on ICOs. South Korea is also exploring the creation of a central bank digital currency (CBDC).

6. India: India's stance on cryptocurrencies has been somewhat fluctuating. While there's no outright ban, the government has expressed concerns about cryptocurrencies' potential for misuse. The Reserve Bank of India (RBI) had previously imposed a ban on bank dealings with crypto-related firms, which was later overturned by the Supreme Court. The government is considering a new regulatory framework.

7. Switzerland: Known for its progressive stance on financial matters, Switzerland has established itself as a hub for cryptocurrency and blockchain innovation. The Swiss approach is characterized by a supportive regulatory environment, with guidelines that facilitate ICOs and crypto trading while ensuring investor protection and AML compliance.

8. Singapore: Singapore has positioned itself as a global cryptocurrency hub, adopting a permissive

and clear regulatory framework. The Monetary Authority of Singapore (MAS) regulates cryptocurrencies and ICOs, ensuring that they comply with AML/CFT regulations. Singapore is also exploring the potential of CBDCs.

9. Australia: Australia treats cryptocurrencies as legal property, subjecting them to capital gains tax. The Australian Transaction Reports and Analysis Centre (AUSTRAC) oversees cryptocurrency exchanges, mandating compliance with AML/CFT regulations.

10. Russia: Russia has a complex relationship with cryptocurrencies. While it has recognized them as taxable property, it prohibits their use as a means of payment. Russian authorities are working on more comprehensive regulations to address the legal status of cryptocurrencies and related activities.

Each country's approach reflects its priorities, whether they are financial stability, consumer protection, innovation facilitation, or a combination of these. The global regulatory landscape for cryptocurrencies continues to evolve as governments seek to balance the benefits of this new technology with the need to mitigate its risks.

Challenges and Progress:

Regulating a decentralized and global phenomenon like cryptocurrencies presents unique challenges for governments, regulatory bodies, and international organizations. The inherent properties of cryptocurrencies and their underlying technology, blockchain, pose significant hurdles in creating effective regulatory frameworks. Here some of the key difficulties, along with the progress being made in addressing them:

Challenges:

1. Decentralization: The lack of a central authority in cryptocurrency networks makes regulation difficult. Traditional financial systems are regulated through institutions like banks, but cryptocurrencies operate on a peer-to-peer basis, complicating oversight and enforcement.

2. Global Nature: Cryptocurrencies transcend national borders, allowing for rapid international transactions. This global reach makes it challenging for any single country to enforce regulations effectively, as activities can easily shift to more permissive jurisdictions.

3. Anonymity and Privacy: While not all cryptocurrencies offer complete anonymity, some like Monero and Zcash are designed for privacy, complicating efforts to trace transactions and identify parties involved in illicit activities.

4. Technological Evolution: The fast pace of technological innovation in the crypto space outstrips the slower regulatory processes. New products and services constantly emerge, often exploiting regulatory grey areas.

5. Lack of Standardization: The absence of global regulatory standards leads to a fragmented landscape where regulations vary widely across different jurisdictions. This inconsistency can hinder international cooperation and enforcement.

6. Enforcement and Compliance: Ensuring compliance with regulations by entities operating in the cryptocurrency space is challenging, especially when these entities might not have a physical presence or clear legal status.

7. Understanding and Expertise: Regulating a complex and technical field requires deep understanding and expertise. Many regulatory bodies struggle to keep

up with the technical aspects of blockchain and cryptocurrencies.

8. Balancing Innovation and Regulation: Finding the right balance between fostering technological innovation and ensuring consumer protection and financial stability is a delicate task. Over-regulation could stifle innovation, while under-regulation might lead to increased risk.

Progress:

Despite these challenges, significant progress has been made in addressing the regulatory needs of the cryptocurrency market:

1. Developing Regulatory Frameworks: Countries around the world are increasingly recognizing the need for and implementing cryptocurrency regulations, focusing on AML, KYC, and consumer protection.

2. International Cooperation: Organizations like the Financial Action Task Force (FATF) are working to develop global standards for cryptocurrency regulation, promoting cooperation among nations.

3. Advancements in Technology for Monitoring: Technological tools for analyzing blockchain transactions are becoming more sophisticated, aiding in the detection of illicit activities.

4. Education and Training: There is a growing focus on educating regulators and law enforcement agencies about cryptocurrencies and blockchain technology.

5. Engagement with Industry Stakeholders: Regulators are increasingly engaging with cryptocurrency businesses, experts, and academia to understand the nuances of the technology and its implications.

6. Exploring Central Bank Digital Currencies (CBDCs): Many countries are researching or developing CBDCs, which could offer some of the benefits of cryptocurrencies while remaining under regulatory purview.
7. Creating Sandboxes and Innovation Hubs: Some jurisdictions have established regulatory sandboxes and innovation hubs to allow for the testing of crypto-related services in a controlled environment.
8. Public Awareness Campaigns: Efforts are being made to educate the public about the risks and benefits of cryptocurrencies, which is crucial for consumer protection.

In summary, while the regulation of decentralized and global phenomena like cryptocurrencies is fraught with challenges, concerted efforts at both the national and international levels are underway to address these issues. The key lies in finding a balance that protects consumers and the financial system without stifling innovation.

Chapter 10: Safeguarding the Future

Future of Cryptocurrency Security:

The future of cryptocurrency security is being shaped by several emerging technologies and practices. Here are some key areas of development:

1. Integration with IoT and AI: The combination of blockchain with Internet of Things (IoT) and Artificial Intelligence (AI) is set to revolutionize various sectors by enhancing data security. This integration is particularly promising in areas such as supply chain management, healthcare systems, and smart cities where data security is crucial.

2. Increased Regulation and Compliance: There's a growing trend towards increased regulation and compliance in the cryptocurrency industry. Governments and regulatory bodies are developing frameworks to govern these decentralized systems, focusing on protecting investors, preventing fraud, and ensuring market stability. Compliance measures like Know Your Customer (KYC) and Anti-Money Laundering (AML) are becoming more common.

3. Adoption by Traditional Finance: Traditional financial institutions are beginning to embrace blockchain technology, integrating it into their operations to improve transparency, security, and efficiency. This adoption indicates the potential of blockchain to transform financial transactions.

4. Metaverse and Web 3.0 Applications: The emergence of the metaverse and Web 3.0 applications represents a new frontier for crypto

security. These technologies rely on decentralized networks and smart contracts, necessitating robust security measures to ensure safe transactions in these virtual environments.

5. Biometric Authentication: The use of biometrics for authentication in cryptocurrency wallets is gaining traction. This approach adds a layer of security beyond traditional passwords, with hardware wallets integrating biometric data for access control.

6. Blockchain Consensus Mechanisms: Innovations like Proof of Stake (PoS) are more energy-efficient and secure against certain attacks. Sharding, which breaks down blockchain data into smaller pieces, improves scalability and network security.

7. Smart Contract Auditing and Formal Verification: As decentralized applications and DeFi platforms grow, auditing and formal verification of smart contracts are becoming crucial. These tools help identify vulnerabilities and bugs, reducing the risk of exploitable code.

8. Quantum-Resistant Cryptography: The advancement of quantum computing poses a threat to current cryptographic systems. Quantum-resistant cryptography is being developed to counteract these threats, although it is still in its early stages.

9. Privacy Coins and Anonymity Solutions: Cryptocurrencies like Monero and Zcash offer enhanced anonymity features, providing a layer of security for users seeking privacy in their transactions.

10. Role of Regulation in Crypto Security: Regulatory frameworks are being established to protect consumers, ensure compliance, and prevent illicit activities. AML and KYC regulations are critical in this aspect, requiring adherence by exchanges and service providers.

These developments indicate a dynamic and evolving landscape in cryptocurrency security, driven by technological advancements and the need for robust protective measures against a backdrop of increasing cyber threats.

The Role of Education and Awareness:

Education and awareness play a crucial role in preventing cryptocurrency crimes. As the adoption of cryptocurrencies increases, so does the potential for various types of fraud, scams, and other malicious activities. Here are key points emphasizing the importance of user education in this context:

1. Understanding the Technology: Many users engage with cryptocurrencies without fully understanding the underlying technology. Education can help users comprehend blockchain technology, how cryptocurrencies work, and the risks associated with digital assets. This understanding is vital for making informed decisions and recognizing potential scams.
2. Recognizing Scams and Frauds: The cryptocurrency space is ripe for various scams, including phishing attacks, Ponzi schemes, and fraudulent ICOs (Initial Coin Offerings). Educating users about common types of scams and their warning signs can significantly reduce the likelihood of falling victim to such crimes.
3. Safe Practices for Storage and Transactions: Users often lack knowledge about secure practices for storing and transacting cryptocurrencies. Education on the use of hardware wallets, the importance of

private key management, and safe transaction practices can enhance individual security.

4. Impact of Regulatory Knowledge: Understanding the regulatory environment of cryptocurrencies in different jurisdictions can help users stay compliant with laws and regulations, reducing the risk of legal issues and inadvertently participating in illegal activities.

5. Promoting Responsible Investment: Cryptocurrencies can be highly volatile, and uninformed investment decisions can lead to significant losses. Education on responsible investment practices, like diversification and understanding market trends, is crucial for protecting users from financial harm.

6. Combating Social Engineering Attacks: Many crypto crimes involve social engineering tactics where criminals manipulate individuals into divulging sensitive information or making unauthorized transactions. Awareness and education on how to recognize and resist these tactics are key to preventing such breaches.

7. Community Involvement and Peer Education: Building a community that values education and awareness can have a multiplying effect. Experienced users sharing their knowledge and insights can foster a more secure and informed cryptocurrency environment.

8. Leveraging Educational Resources: Utilizing available resources such as online courses, webinars, community forums, and educational content from reputable sources can significantly boost a user's ability to navigate the cryptocurrency world safely.

In summary, education and awareness are pivotal in equipping users with the knowledge and skills needed to navigate the cryptocurrency landscape safely and responsibly. This approach is not just about individual protection but also about building a more secure and trustworthy cryptocurrency ecosystem.

Conclusion

The Balancing Act:

The need to balance innovation with safety and regulation in the realm of cryptocurrency and blockchain technology is a critical challenge. This balancing act involves encouraging technological advancements and economic growth while ensuring consumer protection, financial stability, and compliance with laws. Here are some key aspects to consider:

1. Fostering Innovation: Cryptocurrencies and blockchain technology represent a significant innovation in financial technology, offering benefits such as decentralization, transparency, and efficiency. It's important to support and nurture this innovation to explore its full potential in various sectors, including finance, supply chain management, healthcare, and more.
2. Ensuring Consumer Protection: As these technologies evolve, so do the risks associated with them, such as fraud, scams, and volatility. Regulatory frameworks need to focus on protecting consumers from these risks, ensuring that their investments and personal data are safe.
3. Maintaining Financial Stability: The integration of cryptocurrencies into the broader financial system poses challenges in maintaining financial stability. Regulators need to understand and monitor the impact of digital assets on financial markets to prevent systemic risks.

4. Compliance and Regulation: Effective regulation is essential to prevent illicit activities such as money laundering and financing of terrorism. However, overregulation can stifle innovation. Hence, a balanced approach is needed where regulations are clear, fair, and adaptable to technological changes.

5. Encouraging Responsible Innovation: Encouraging companies to engage in responsible innovation involves ensuring that they consider the security, privacy, and ethical implications of their technologies. This approach helps in building trust among users and investors.

6. International Collaboration: Cryptocurrencies operate on a global scale, making international collaboration crucial for effective regulation. Harmonizing regulatory approaches across different jurisdictions can help manage cross-border challenges.

7. Education and Awareness: Educating both regulators and the public about the nuances of blockchain and cryptocurrencies is vital. Well-informed regulators can create more effective policies, and educated consumers can make safer decisions.

8. Balancing Privacy and Transparency: Blockchain offers enhanced privacy but also raises concerns about transparency and traceability. Finding a balance between protecting user privacy and ensuring sufficient transparency for regulatory purposes is essential.

Looking Ahead:

1. Looking ahead, the future of cryptocurrencies and their role in society is multifaceted and evolving. Cryptocurrencies have transitioned from digital novelties to technologies with significant market value and the potential to disrupt the global financial system. They are increasingly seen as assets and are used for a variety of transactions, ranging from legal to illicit activities.

2. Proponents of cryptocurrencies view them as democratizing forces that shift the power of money creation and control away from central banks and traditional financial institutions. They are praised for their potential to increase financial inclusion and decentralization. However, critics highlight the challenges, including their use in criminal activities, market volatility, and environmental concerns due to high energy consumption.

3. Regulatory approaches to cryptocurrencies vary globally, with some governments embracing them and others imposing bans or limitations. Many countries, including the United States, are exploring or developing their own central bank digital currencies (CBDCs) to compete with the growing popularity of decentralized cryptocurrencies.

4. Overall, the future of cryptocurrencies is likely to be shaped by a complex interplay of innovation, regulation, technological advancements, and societal acceptance.

In summary:

Education and awareness are vital in safeguarding users against cryptocurrency crimes. Understanding the technology, recognizing scams, practicing safe storage and transaction methods, comprehending regulatory environments, making informed investment decisions, resisting social engineering attacks, and leveraging community knowledge are key. Educated users are better equipped to navigate the crypto landscape safely and contribute to a secure ecosystem.

Cryptocurrencies have evolved from digital curiosities to significant technologies with the potential to disrupt global finance. They offer democratization of financial systems but also pose challenges like market volatility and criminal use. Regulatory responses vary globally, with many countries considering or developing central bank digital currencies (CBDCs) to compete with decentralized cryptocurrencies. The future of cryptocurrencies will be shaped by innovation, regulation, societal acceptance, and technological advancements.

A Special Note from Michael McNaught

Dear Reader,

I hope you enjoyed the content of this book and found it informative and helpful. Your thoughts and experience matter greatly. Please consider sharing your review and feedback about each of my books that you have read.

Your feedback is not only immensely valuable to me, but It also helps fellow crypto and blockchain enthusiasts to discover my books.

Thank you for choosing my book. Follow me on fb and X for more exciting and interesting products. Stay Tuned!

Warm regards,

Michael McNaught

facebook.com/MM Bookstore

twitter.com/Mcnaughm1986